The Ballad of Saint Lidoire

Robert K Gardner

"The Ballad of Saint Lidoire"

By

Robert K. Gardner

ISBN-13: 978-1-940122-31-1

Published by Alternative Book Press

The Ballad of Saint Lidoire

Robert K Gardner

The girl Lidoire was born and raised
In fair Provence, a land of wine
And lords of fearsome countenance,
Their ladies' beauty and manners fine.

A good and gracious daughter she
Of a knight who was a mighty lord,
From beneath a wimple white and clean
Her matchless beauty was out poured.

Her limbs like tender saplings' branches,
Her bosom soft and downy white;
Her movements lithe and graceful, she stepped
Through muddy lanes like a fawn might.

Her father's stony castle she kept

The Ballad of Saint Lidoire

In such a manner that a king
Should ever one be waylaid there
Would find his comfort never lacking.

Her mother was a lady Moor
Captured by Frankish knights and brought
From paynim Spain to Christian France.
Of Him our Savior she was taught

And baptized was she soon thereafter.
To him who'd rescued her from darkness
She lost her heart and married soon.
Their coupling met with much success:

A pair of boys then sweet Lidoire.
But O what sorrow came to pass
For in birthing a future saint
The lady mother breathed her last.

As mistress of her father's house
Lidoire was patient, kind, yet stern.
Her women she made ply their needles,

Robert K Gardner

Her cooks their wits so not to burn

The stew, her varlets their legs to fetch
Some needful person or thing to her.
Though dreary sometimes was her work,
Joyless it was you mustn't infer,

For nothing did she love as much
As overseeing the vineyard;
And bare of foot and light of heart,
She flitted through it like a bird.

The season of the grape was wont
To be hot; as a consequence
The workers stripped as much as they could
While still avoiding decadence.

Indeed, Lidoire was known to walk
About the vineyard wearing but
The shortest dress, like a chemise,
Without a girdle, of shocking cut,

7

The Ballad of Saint Lidoire

And not a hint of petticoat.
On days too hot she liked to rest
Upon a shaded chair and often
She slept, her chin curled on her breast.

Although by inclination not
Intemperate, so many were the days
Her sleep was deeper made by the cups
Of wine the men and she would raise.

One early autumn day Lidoire
Was stricken with a stomach ailment.
Her monthly blood had stopped as well,
Though she'd been ever abstinent.

Her troubling state she hid as well
As possible from her doting maids;
But hard it was from those who groomed
And bathed her, dressed her, and set her braids.

The whispering swirled about Lidoire
But nothing reached her father's ears;

For none would risk his wrath to tell

Come true had one of his greatest fears:

His girl disgraced, the one he'd pledged

To marry the prince of Navarre--

His fury would be legendary.

A tearful harvest wept Lidoire.

When swollen belly she could hide

No more, to her a visitor came.

Into her chamber he humbly walked,

His weathered face with care aflame.

"My dear Lidoire, what's happened to you?"

The man, her father's vintner, cried.

To her he'd been as near an uncle

As possible. To him she sighed,

Then sadly answered. "A mystery

To me it truly is, Moreau.

I've never lain with any man.

Whose child this is I do not know.

"I dare not think but wonder still:
How like to Mary's plight is mine.
No angel appeared and spoke to me,
However; heaven sent no sign."

"What didn't come from heaven must needs
Have come from Earth," Moreau declared.
"I'll be your sign so come with me.
From your father's wrath I'd see you spared."

"I think that fleeing would confirm
My guilt when I am innocent.
My dear Moreau, I'll stay at home
And here to father's judgment consent."

"I fear for you, my dear Lidoire,
And would not see you put away.
You'll get no judgment fair now that
Your father's scheme has gone astray."

"Wherever would we flee?" she asked

Moreau, distressed, "and to what end?
"Wherever you put me pregnant I'll
Remain. That tear you cannot mend."

"I'll put you in a hermitage,
Away until the child is born.
The monk's my kin; with him you'll stay
Till blooms again the yellow hawthorn."

"And what will happen then?" she asked.
"To your worried father you'll return
With his grandchild at suck. He'll be
So pleased that you he will not spurn."

"And you'll remain at father's house?"
She asked, hoping with her he'd stay.
"Expect me early spring," he said.
"Come, ride we must. No more delay!"

Lidoire, her head still full of doubts,
Rode out that very night. He took
Her north to a wild wood. The known

The Ballad of Saint Lidoire

And trodden paths he both forsook.

The hermitage they finally reached
And Moreau's brother the monk they met.
His dwelling was a simple lodge
That made Lidoire begin to fret.

"This place is hardly fit for one
With child," she said to Moreau aside.
"So cold and rainy are our winters.
What in this forest will us betide?"

"Whatever is the will of God
Will happen to you, my pretty lady,"
Moreau's brother the monk replied.
"Regarding the cold, I'm sure you see

The wealth of brush and trees around
And can imagine very plain
The wealth of kindling contained therein.
A certain cadence has the rain

As it patters my humble roof,

But howsoever it may knock

Admittance it shall never gain:

The thatch's as solid as a rock."

"But who's to help me birth my child?

Around me I'll have no womenfolk.

Why did I leave my father's house?"

Moreau it was this time who spoke.

"The work is mostly yours whether

You had a gaggle of maidens near

Or not. No one can pull it out

For you. You'll have to push, I fear."

"To jest like that is cruel," she cried.

Moreau made his apology.

Lidoire refused to listen. The monk

With kindly physiognomy

Sat down beside the weeping girl,

And spoke to her in soothing tones:

The Ballad of Saint Lidoire

"Though I'm no maid, some knowledge of
Birthing has seeped into these bones.

And something more I know: The Lord
Does nothing ever here in vain.
We're here together for a reason,
For His glory and our lesser gain."

The monk thus mollified Lidoire.
Moreau of them then took his leave.
Before he could, however, the monk
Prevented him by catching his sleeve.

"Whose daughter is she?" he asked Moreau,
"And who has graced her with his seed?
And do not tell me that it's you,
Though I suspect you did this deed.

I'm pleased to see you, but to bring
With you some noble's pregnant daughter,
That I might hide her through the winter,
Sustain her on nuts and riverwater...

O rash, improvident Moreau!"
That rogue replied: "This girl, you see,
Despite her belly is a virgin.
In her tale a monk like you should glory."

Moreau then spurred his horse and ignored
His brother's warning to refrain
From adding blasphemy to the sins
That form on his soul an ugly stain.

Moreau returned to Lidoire's father.
Word of her flight then quickly spread.
The rumors all had come to light.
Heavy they weighed on her father's head.

The autumn passed. The weather turned.
A cold and rainy mist hung low
Over Provence and often it rained.
Lidoire was pleased there'd been no snow;

For as her belly grew the lodge

The Ballad of Saint Lidoire

Shrank--seemingly in equal measure.
The monk demanded much of her.
Lidoire had little time for leisure.

The days she spent in fetching wood
And making nut and berry paste,
The nights in praying with the monk
While for sleep waiting to be embraced.

These hardships she could countenance
But not his tendency to pry.
He urged her to unburden herself
To him, and with a kindly sigh,

Assured her that the heavy heart
She surely carried in her breast
Would be lightened if she but shared.
So for her father's name he pressed,

From whence she came, and how she knew
His brother Moreau as well. Demurely,
Lidoire declined. The monk persisted.

Robert K Gardner

His questions must have an end, surely,

She thought. How long can he continue
To vex and importune me thus?
She wavered, nearly told him all,
Thinking: Out here there's only us.

What harm if he my story knows?
He is a man of God, beside.
But wise Lidoire resisted and
In silence she chose to abide.

The monk while foraging one day
Encountered a man upon his mount.
So rare were travelers, of his
Journey the monk asked some account.

The rider was in search of a girl,
The daughter of a knight of Provence,
Who promised to the prince of Navarre,
Was pregnant by amorous mischance

The Ballad of Saint Lidoire

By a lover with whom she'd fled.
Her father's riders crossed the land
Looking for sign or word of her.
The monk on hearing quickly planned

To bring Lidoire to her father's house,
And win his gratitude and praise,
"And more than a few sous," he thought,
His latent greed now set ablaze.

In truth the monk was such a man
Who could resist all temptation
Until the time that he was tempted.
Easier was his monk's vocation

When in the woods so far from women,
And wine, the wealth of lords and kings.
He presently returned to the lodge
And spoke to Lidoire of many things

That were though seemingly sundry
Subtly crafted to make his point:

Robert K Gardner

To have the baby here--that was
Unsafe, and she should now appoint

Him her protector, humble guide
Back to her father's warm embrace.
By dint of her maternal fears
Lidoire was able to efface

Her own objections on taking such
A journey long in her condition.
She hesitated still, however,
Until the monk made this admission:

"The art of the midwife's unknown
To me," he said, and he was lying.
Lidoire then told him all and they
Set off, the tears that she was crying,

Of joy at seeing home again,
The glint in the eye of the monk
Evincing a desire for coins,
Enough to fill the largest trunk.

The Ballad of Saint Lidoire

Lidoire and the monk agreed to say
Nothing about Moreau and the part
He played in helping her escape.
She feared for him inside her heart.

They rested often and traveled quick
Until they saw her father's gates.
But for Lidoire, no warm embrace,
For her no place by the hearth awaits.

Her father, on hearing her tale,
Had poor Lidoire taken away.
To the monk he gave a letter meant
For the bishop, and meant to sway

That worthy priest into taking
The monk into his retinue.
The brother of Moreau thus leaves
Our tale for ease and wealth. Adieu!

Lidoire was locked away in her rooms

Robert K Gardner

For days before a visitor came:
The priest who'd baptized her mother and her,
A righteous one of great acclaim.

In joy to see another, Lidoire
Fell to her knees and clasped her hands.
"Tell me my father's mind," she cried,
"And what he says are his demands."

"Rise, child, and wipe your eyes. He asks
That you relate to me the truth.
Your father is both stern and just,
But there in him remains some ruth."

Straightening her skirt, Lidoire arose
And with a noble bearing spoke:
"My tale remains unchanged," she said.
The truth I've never tried to cloak."

"In all my years--and there've been many--
A girl has never tried to pass
A tale like yours, my dear, as truth.

The Ballad of Saint Lidoire

I know you're lying; it's clear as glass."

"Lying I'm not and you I pity
If getting me to you've been tasked."
"Then you have no idea whose seed
You carry?" full of doubt he asked.

"I've no idea," Lidoire replied.
"Would you," he asked, "consent to allow
A splinter of the Cross to prick
One finger as this you avow?"

She did and then the priest produced
That sharp and holy wooden sliver.
Her fingernail he stabbed beneath
Until with pain she went aquiver.

Lidoire, affrighted, sobbed and wept.
"You told me one finger you'd prick,"
She managed to protest. "Be still,
And think of Mary--that is the trick."

She did and then as soon as it
Had come the pain retreated from her;
And though the priest stabbed all her nails,
Lidoire's tears dried. She didn't stir,

As she avowed she knew not who
Had put the child inside her womb.
Amazed, the priest stepped back from her,
And came rushing into the room,

The people listening at the door.
"A witch she is," one cried. "Enchanted!"
Another. "Neither," said the priest.
"Though this is passing strange," he granted.

"To her father we must bring her now,"
Commanded he. They seized her then.
They rushed her to her father's hall
Where he was sitting with his brethren.

The priest recounted the events,
Declaring Lidoire, in misery,

The Ballad of Saint Lidoire

Had spoken true about the father.

"His name's to be a mystery?"

Her father asked, incredulous.

"I think that she's protecting the knave.

She doesn't want to see me put

The fool into an early grave."

"I had no lover, father dear.

I didn't know the seed's presence

Till after it was sown in me."

"Lidoire, if you had any sense,

Then you'd refrain from lying to me,"

He said. "You think that I believe

Your maidenhead could broken be

And that a child you could conceive

Without your knowledge?" he demanded.

"Speak now, Lidoire! And do not prattle."

"Do you recall my maidenhead

Was taken by a horse's saddle?"

Robert K Gardner

The hall erupted in laughter till
Lidoire's father threatened their tongues
With removal swift, and painful too.
Portentously, he filled his lungs

In preparation to speak to her.
"You disobeyed me then the same,"
He said. "I would not let you ride
To protect your thin and girlish frame."

"When young, my mother rode upon
The finest Spanish horses there were,"
She said. "You told me that yourself.
I shared the riding passion with her."

Her father fell to studying her,
The double of his lovely wife,
Her pretty face, her tall straight back,
Enchanting eyes, her mind like a knife,

Her belly ornamenting the whole.

The Ballad of Saint Lidoire

If she were someone else, the whip
She'd feel for speaking thus to me,
He thought, my heart is in her grip.

The priest then chose this time to speak.
"I think there's something else at work,
My lord: demonic possession.
I think an evil seems to lurk

Inside this hitherto good girl,
Inside her comely form and face."
"I'm quite alone in here," Lidoire
Rejoined, "excepting this one place."

She cupped her swollen belly and smiled.
"A demon, lord, will try to lull you,"
The priest declared. "All manner of
Denials, lies, and falsehoods they'll spew

In tones most soothing, kind, and sweet."
"An evil in her I do not sense,"
Lidoire's poor father replied, "but I'm

Robert K Gardner

No priest and wouldn't have it said hence

That I neglected my daughter's soul
And let a demon therein dwell."
"Father, I beg you! Reconsider!
There is no demon to expel."

"Precisely what a demon would say,"
The priest rejoined. "Everyone knows,"
Lidoire replied, "when you a demon
Expel, the human's life, too, goes."

"Silence, you foul and fiendish beast.
You might have sinned with this girl's flesh.
You might speak bold and brazenly.
Your evil with her you did enmesh,

But I will disentangle you!"
Lidoire rushed to her father's chair
And knelt to rest her chin on his knee.
He put his hand onto her hair.

The Ballad of Saint Lidoire

"My lord," the priest intoned, "heed not
A thing it says. This girl is not your girl."
"Papa, I swear on all that's holy,"
Lidoire said, looking up, a curl

Of hair upon her rosy cheek.
"There is no demon possessing me."
"Then why this change in you?" he asked.
"With a bastard pregnant, then you flee?

And now you won't reveal the man
Who caused your abject, hopeless shame?
Lidoire, this isn't you. Tell me,"
He asked the priest, "how will you tame

This demon inside my dear Lidoire?
Why did your splinter fail to drive
Him out?" "Because it's but a splinter.
No matter how hard that I might strive,

I still have only a piece of The Cross.
A plank of it would drive him out,

Perhaps. He's very powerful.

The might of Christ he's able to flout."

"Well what do you propose to do

To my Lidoire?" asked her father.

"The demon must be forced from her,"

The priest replied. "My lord, I'd rather

I knew some other, gentler way

To do this but none is known to me.

A demon's element is fire,

And so to cause this one to flee

Her form, they both must be submerged

Within its opposite: water.

And to ensure this demon drowns

And doesn't just escape your daughter

To plague some other Christian girl,

Lidoire must be sewn in a sack

Before we give her to the river."

"Oh father, put me on the rack,"

The Ballad of Saint Lidoire

Our poor Lidoire cried. "Pluck my eyes
And take from me my very sight;
But, papa dear, I beg of you
To never seal me from the light

To thrash about and drown in darkness."
"The soul of she and of her child,"
Declared the priest, "will be in heaven
And with The Lord be reconciled.

As Jesus said 'the Spirit gives
Life and the flesh counts not at all.'"
Easy to say of someone else,
Reflected her father standing tall

And saying with evident regret
"I'll have it done as this priest said."
Lidoire, still sitting at his feet,
Said quietly, "then I am dead."

A single voice then cried aloud.

A commotion ensued wherein
A man had pushed his way to the front.
Lidoire's voice sounded above the din.

"Moreau," she cried. "Hear me, my lord,"
He said, "and let the father speak."
"You found him?" Lidoire's father asked.
"I have!" Lidoire let loose a shriek.

Her father rushed down to Moreau.
"Where did you find him? What's his name?"
"I found him in this very hall
And he and I are called the same."

"Produce him now or plainly speak!"
Lidoire's father cried, shaking him.
"No jests or riddles more from you!"
His eyes were wild, his look was grim.

"I shall," he said, "the child is mine."
"That cannot be, you fool, Moreau!"
Her father cried. "For whom do you lie?

The Ballad of Saint Lidoire

You're not the father--that I know."

"My lord, I tell you it was me."
"No!" cried Lidoire. "You were just like
A kind and loving uncle to me."
"Whose head will soon adorn a spike,"

He answered with the saddest smile.
"An uncle who fell deep in love
With the girl then woman you became."
"Moreau, I swear to God above,"

Lidoire's father with wrath declared,
"I'll hang you myself, if this be true."
Lidoire cried simply, "Why, oh, why?"
And feeling violated anew.

Moreau then told his sordid tale:
Of how Lidoire's décolletage,
And narrow shoulders, slender calves,
And pretty smile, like a mirage

Robert K Gardner

In a homely desert, caught his eye,
His fancy; how her airs, so humble
And sweet where in another they'd
Be cruel and haughty, caused to crumble

What judgment he had; of how her skill
And wisdom beyond her precious years
In keeping her father's busy house
Reduced this man to foolish tears;

Of how the thought that she should be
Wed soon and be forever out
Of reach, be taken by another,
Made him his sanity to doubt.

"No man could love her as I could,"
Moreau finished. Within the hall
No sounds there were except Lidoire,
Whose angry sobbing cast a pall.

"You speak so prettily, Moreau,"
She finally said through sobs, "but more

The Ballad of Saint Lidoire

I'd know: Just how without my knowledge,
You took me like a common whore?"

"My dear Lidoire, a whore you're not--"
"The act!" she cried. "Tell me, Moreau."
When dressed so scantily she slumbered
In that vineyard chair, her skin aglow,

She slouched in such a way that his
Deflowering of her was made
Inevitable. "And you were drunk,"
He added, quietly, dismayed.

"I always used to wonder why,"
She said, "you wished the wine to flow,
Never imagining it was
So you the seed of betrayal could sow."

Moreau then tried to plead with her,
But she, her tears all dry, slapped him.
"And I'm to raise your bastard child?"
She cried, "our futures both are dim."

Robert K Gardner

She parted those who gawked at her
As running heedless she left the hall.
Her father, drained from the secrets told,
Steadied himself against a wall.

"My lord?" the priest inquired at length,
"These revelations must not delay
Action against this horrid fiend.
We must act quick! This very day!"

"My dear Lidoire was plied with wine
And raped," he angrily replied.
"The only demon is in Moreau."
"My lord, to you your daughter lied

And hid her belly from your eyes.
She fled--O what dishonesty!"
"Drown someone else's girl, some fool
Who'll heed your vicious sophistry.

One death this day is quite enough."

The Ballad of Saint Lidoire

Lidoire's poor father gestured for
His guards to lock Moreau away.
About Lidoire he said no more.

Indeed, that lady hid herself
All while the gallows was being built.
(Moreau had hoped to die a noble's
Death, his blood by the headsman spilt

Instead of hanged like a common thief.)
Lidoire was never seen till Moreau
Stood with the rope around his neck.
Atop the gallows perched a crow.

Her plumage black as well, Lidoire
Was seen to move about the courtyard.
Though veiled, the people knew their lady.
Her way to the gallows no one barred.

Indeed, as through the crowd she passed
The people gathered made a path.
A hush fell over them as they

Awaited some new sign of wrath.

Atop the gallows steps, her father
Attempted stopping her from mounting.
With just a look, she stopped him cold.
Of his diffidence there's no accounting.

Though greatly loved by father dear,
With discipline Lidoire'd been raised.
For her obedience and depth
Of curtsy, father dear'd been praised.

That day it was her father timid
As daughter did whatever she would.
Her veil she raised, then ordered the
Hangman to raise Moreau's black hood.

To him she said, "Moreau, I want
The final face you see to be mine."
And in his haunted, vacant eyes
A calm appeared as if from wine.

The Ballad of Saint Lidoire

"Forgive me," he said, his voice a rasp.
"I do," she said."Have mercy on me."
"May God have mercy on your soul."
"A taste of water, dearest lady,

My final one." "The only water
I have I'll share with you." She stood
Upon her toes and kissed his mouth.
"To judgment send him, if you would,"

To the hangman she after said.
She veiled her lovely teary eyes
As poor Moreau was forced to don
The hood--to his evident surprise!

He struggled a time against his bonds
And lolled his head from side to side
But the noose was soon around his neck.
The name Lidoire he once more cried.

The gallows she already was
With sobs and anger hastening from.

Robert K Gardner

With naught but air beneath his feet,
Moreau was rendered forever dumb.

The son of Moreau was sent to kin,
A sister with children of her own.
Though other marriage offers came,
The heart of Lidoire was God's alone;

For she had prayed and He had called.
Unlike the man who wouldn't leave
His wealth behind to follow Christ,
She parted with hers without a thought.

Though wroth at losing his precious pawn
In the marriage alliance game,
Her father didn't prevent her vows
And on his family bring more shame.

Behind the abbey walls she went
And lived full 20 years in prayer,
Doing the things that saints are wont
To do, which peasants love to hear.

The Ballad of Saint Lidoire

Her son was kept from her until
The day he came to the abbey gate.
He'd taken up the Cross and in
The Holy Land did lay his fate.

He learned of his mother recently
When Moreau's sister, sick in bed
And nearing death, informed the son
His mother lived and wasn't dead.

Her vows would not allow Lidoire
To speak at all to even her son.
The abbess took pity on her,
And told her she needn't fully shun

This boy unlawfully begot,
Now pilgrim to the Holy Land.
Lidoire she told to hasten to
The garden wall, and there to stand

Where the abbey walls were very low

And not a woman's hand breadth thick.
And even though they couldn't see,
Through crumbling mortar and thin brick

They could converse. And that they did,
Mother and son on either side
Of that mossy, old, and dreary wall.
And neither one of them could hide

The feelings rising in their voice.
They spoke of sundry little things
Except the sorrow and bitter pain
That lasting separation brings;

For Lidoire was old and went her son
Where many men had gone and not
Returned. Whether from pestilence
Or wounds, their glory was dearly bought.

Lidoire then asked if a girl had caught
His heart and given him some favor,
Some ribbon, stocking, token of love

The Ballad of Saint Lidoire

That he in trying times could savor.

"I'll tie no stocking around my lance
Nor any ribbon on my coat.
The sentimental fool does that--
Might as well wear a petticoat."

"You're far too young to be so stern,"
She said. "But ah, your blood for battle
Is raging hot like all young men's.
You hate to hear a mother's prattle.

"I pray that you live long enough
To value love as women do.
Even as girls we know the power
Of love. Your wretched father knew."

"Speak not of him!" he cried aloud.
"A bastard penniless he made me.
No armor, horse, or land have I.
He ruined you and made you flee

Robert K Gardner

The splendid life awaiting you
To rot behind these dismal walls."
Lidoire reflected quietly.
The only sounds the birds and their calls.

"And yet I wish that I could speak
To him," she answered, "just once more,
To have some time in father's vineyard
And wear again those clothes I wore.

Our time is passing, dearest boy,
And you and me and poor Moreau
Will be forgotten memories.
Dead will be everyone we know."

"I hope that you would want to speak
To him only to curse him more."
"Our Lord commanded us to forgive
Four hundred, ninety times; before"

Attempting such a feat, I say
We--truly--forgive a single trespass,

The Ballad of Saint Lidoire

And we'll discover what's beyond
Forgiveness, and blessings we'll amass."

"Moreau's deeds are beyond forgiveness."
"What lies beyond forgiveness is love.
It covers my thoughts and entire soul
Like the hand enveloped by the glove.

"As hard as it is to hear, my son,
I could have loved that wretch Moreau."
Lidoire's son rose to leave her there.
"That splendid life I never knew,"

She cried, "how splendid was it truly?
The man I was to marry turned out
To be unfaithful, stingy, cruel,
And known to give his wife a clout

If she but sipped her wine too loud.
A child she lost after this beast
Beat her senseless. Moreau the poor
Besotted fool, loved me at least.

Robert K Gardner

Sharing a bed with such a man,

One forced on me, would be much worse

Than the sin Moreau committed that day,

Bearing his children would be a curse,"

And more than one the beast would want.

Whatever beauty I possessed

Would disappear beneath his blows.

For freedom, I'd plunge a knife in my breast."

"I leave you now," her son declared.

"Wait, son! If there's no maiden favor

You'll wear, wear one from she who was

A maiden once--and God's disfavor

May never you earn while wearing this."

The simple ribbon that kept her hair

From falling about her face and eyes,

The only adornment that she'd wear,

She flung over the wall to him.

The Ballad of Saint Lidoire

He took it, bid Lidoire farewell,

And didn't think of it until

Jerusalem, itself a shell

From the fighting between the Christian

And Saracen. With the forces

Of Godfrey de Bouillon he'd gone,

The knights atop their mighty horses,

The thousands following on foot.

They'd laid siege to the Holy City.

Outside the walls the armies suffered

Enough to move a heart to pity.

Starvation and thirst bedeviled them.

A priest then had a holy vision

In which God pledged the city's fall.

If around the walls they made procession

Barefoot and meek, in fewer than nine

Days the Christians would be inside.

The son of Lidoire then found the ribbon.

Robert K Gardner

His bitter tears he couldn't hide.

He tied it to the simple robe
He wore as singing and praying
He circled the holy city's walls
With his fellows, all of them obeying

The vision; and soon Jerusalem
Was safe again in Christian hands.
When Godfrey's standards were proudly raised
And he subdued surrounding lands

This great and pious duke recalled
Who in the siege had proven brave.
The son of poor Lidoire was brought
And to that worthy man he gave

In fief some lands in timber rich
And olives. About his battle cry
The duke inquired. "A woman's name
You shouted loud to terrify

The Ballad of Saint Lidoire

The Saracens atop the walls.
Who is this woman Lidoire to you?"
"A saint of my homeland, my lord,
Who has to me been ever true.

Before we took the walls, I prayed
That she might help me deliver
Jerusalem from paynim hands;
And she it was who set aquiver

The hearts of the defenders when
Like a mighty crashing wave your host
Broke on the walls and filled the streets
And harried them to the outmost.

"I mean to build a shrine to her
And in its altar put this relic."
He showed the duke the simple ribbon,
Which in the light, did glow angelic.

"She wore this simple thing," he said
Of his mother, "after she forsook

Robert K Gardner

A wedding dress for the habit
Of a nun. In an abbey nook,

She tied her hair up from her face
Each morning after thanking God
For one more day. She did her work
In simple dress and poorly shod."

"A shrine you shall not build," the duke
Declared. "You'll build instead a church
And dedicate it to this saint.
Her pilgrims won't have far to search:

In sight of The Holy Sepulcher
You'll have the workmen raise the stones
And into chronicles I'll have
Her name emblazoned. You have bones,

A lock of hair, some other relic
Than this ribbon? It's fine, of course,
It's just that pilgrims like remains.
Perhaps the teeth of the mighty horse

The Ballad of Saint Lidoire

She used to ride? Perhaps a tusk
Of the boar she tamed with but her dulcet
Voice or a feather from the eagle
That saw from above she was beset

By demons one dreadful, stormy day
And carried her away to safety?"
"I've something better," said the son
Of poor Lidoire, "I'll bring you she

Herself." The duke considered this.
"The saints reside in heaven, but some
There are alive who are like saints,
And some saints, if the dead weren't dumb,

Would be revealed to us as scoundrels.
This Saint Lidoire is not the latter;
Summon her here and let me see
If she's the former." With a clatter,

The duke arose from his chair and left

Robert K Gardner

The hall. The son of Lidoire then asked
A trusted comrade to go and bring
Lidoire to him. He further tasked

Him to deliver her a note
Sealed with his signet ring on wax
Warning Lidoire to secret keep
His parentage. The journey would tax

Her greatly he feared; he needn't have
Worried at all: Lidoire'd been dead
For days before her son's comrade
Arrived. She'd been confined to bed,

The weeping comrade was informed,
And one night sat up she and cried,
"Jerusalem! Jerusalem!",
The very night her son had tried

To take the city a final time.
And as she closed her eyes on life

The Ballad of Saint Lidoire

The Holy City was Christian,
But not yet free from bloody strife;

For the kingdom of Jerusalem
Knew peace but for the shortest time.
Its wars, betrayals, and intrigues fill
Many a minstrel's song and rhyme.

The church of Saint Lidoire was built
Exactly as the duke had ordered;
Her son long battled the Saracens
Against whose lands his own bordered.

Thus ends this tale of a Frankish girl
Who forgave the grievous trespass of
Another to join the ranks of saints
And learned when least deserved that love

Is truest unto its truest self,
That we must endeavor to go
Beyond notions of right-doing
And wrong if divine love we'd know.